THINK AND GROW WEALTH

HOW THE POOR GET RICH AND HOW THE RICH GET WEALTHY

BY JON ROBERT QUINN

Introduction

Your Job

What is Organization?

Starting Your First Business

Building My First Retail Store

Building a Foundation

Personal Finance

Spenders, Savers and Investors

Stocks

Using OPM

Encouraging Entrepreneurship

Be a Leader

Be Original

Building a Business System

Expect Good Things

Increase Sales by Properly Training Sales People

Happiness

Conclusion

Introduction

Hello, I am Jon Robert Quinn, an entrepreneur, national talk show host, published author and recording artist. In this book, I will talk to you about ways I have used to increase my Wealth, Health and Life. I'm not going to tell you how to get rich quick, rather I will show you ways I have used to get rid of my boring, go nowhere job, start businesses and build a path to financial freedom. I will show you ways on how to get your finances in order and use the investment vehicles available to become a smarter and more efficient entrepreneur and business owner.

If you have read any of my other books, then you probably know my story. I was a kid that grew up in a broken home, was physically abused and a troubled youth with bad grades. I was born in Lakenheath, England to parents both in the Air Force. We came to the states when I was only one. Maybe ten years ago, I was given a file from my childhood and in it were hospital records and it was there I discovered the issues my parents had, started before I was even born. They fought a lot. I remember being a toddler and the toaster flying across the room. When I was five, my mother left to marry my uncle. I was to be raised by my father with an iron fist. I can get into a lot more, but I will save this for another time.

Having such a difficult childhood, I could have made excuses for myself, but I didn't. I worked hard, held myself accountable and made something of myself. When I was in school, I was a terrible student. I think a lot of it was boredom. I hated history, but today I collect American historical artifacts. I spend a lot of my time reading and learning about America's past and why things are the way they are. So why wasn't I interested in school? I never went to college. Neither did my parents, nor my brother or sister.

As a child, my favorite subject was math. I would sit there for hours looking at number patterns with one of my favorites being what I call the power of nines. Take any number between 10 and infinity, add the numbers together and subtract from the sum. It will always equal 9. For instance. 10 (1+0) = 1. Subtract 1 from 10 and you have now have 9. Take 241 as another example. 2+4+1 = 7. Take 7 from 241. You now have 234. 2+3+4 = 9. Why am I telling you this? Because I would sit there for hours as a child looking at numbers, but the schools never challenged me, making school fun providing me a quality education.

Life is a lot like this. Often times, we get into a comfortable situation and take the path of least resistance forgetting to challenge ourselves. This is preventing us from making ourselves stronger and preventing us from become successful. Success doesn't happen unless we continually learn how successful people become successful and how to apply this into our lives. There are a lot of people that read every business book but they fail to apply the information into their life and this prevents those people from creating any REAL success.

I started my first official business at the age of seventeen. Around age fifteen, I started writing music and making cassettes to sell to the kids at school. I remember going to the thrift store and buying books on cassette, then using nail polish remover and erasing the words off the face of the cassettes. I would then apply a piece of tape over the holes at the top and record my music one by one onto each of the cassettes. I would then draw the artwork for each cassette by hand and sign each one. If one of the cassettes didn't sell at school, I would put them on consignment at the local music store. I would call each week asking if any of my cassettes sold and for months, not one sold. After about a year, I called the music shop and was pleasantly surprised that I had five bucks waiting for me at the store.

A couple years would pass, and I felt it was time for me to build a real business. I wanted to get rich and I wanted fast money. Little did I know that fast money usually turns into fast failure. I had no idea where to start. One day, I started by buying and selling cellular phones on eBay. I would purchase used Nokia cellular phones, refurbish them and sell them online and in various places. After about a year, I found myself in a little bit of trouble and was forced to close the business. I knew what I was trying to do but didn't have the skills or discipline to execute it properly. Essentially, I was just another small business statistic, failing after only a couple years in business and leaving behind a ton of debt and bad credit.

It was at that point, I really felt like I needed to focus on my music career. That was where my heart was anyway. I started performing as many shows as I could and was constantly writing and releasing new music. Eventually I would find myself with a manager and making a living traveling playing music professionally. Though I was building in popularity around Northern California and Nevada, I wasn't making any real money and had to rethink where my life was taking me.

A few months would pass, and I met a gentleman carrying a bunch of motorcycle helmets into his apartment. I asked him the story with the helmets and asked how I could become a local dealer and with a little convincing, I started selling motorcycle helmets and accessories for the company. This is what propelled my potential as a business owner.

Though I was only twenty-six years old, I was starting to develop as an entrepreneur by trying new things and not being afraid to make mistakes. I would try one thing, then fail, then try something else. That would succeed and then I'd try something and fail again. Still playing shows several nights a week and selling helmets out of my apartment during the day, things started to make sense. My girlfriend at the time came home from work one day and the house was filled to the ceiling with helmets. Literally hundreds of helmet boxes lined the walls of the apartment. This was when I started taking helmets out to the flea markets. The flea markets were a huge success prompting every motorcycle shop in town to start bringing their inventory out to get a piece of the action.

Eventually I would start opening retail stores. If I knew then what I know now about business, I would probably still own a bunch of successful motorcycle and racing shops.

Months turned into years and years into almost a decade and with the power of the recession of 2008, by 2012 it was all gone. Everything was gone. I took too many risks when I should have been buckling down and only experience will teach you that. I was now homeless and sleeping of a buddy's floor. I chose one day that sleeping in my car was better idea and then with the power of determination, I started my next business… Media.

Notes

Your Job

Most people hate their job. A lot of people love their job. And it's those people who have done their homework and found something that works for them. If you're ready to get rid of your JOB and start a business, whether it's working from home or opening a restaurant, then listen up.

You get up every morning and think "why do I go to work?" Well, it's simple! You must eat. You must feed your family. You must live somewhere and you want nice things. So, you put up with it. Every single day. What if it could be different? You're probably thinking to yourself that you don't have time. Whether you're young or old, have a family or not, there is time to start a business or do something that YOU want to do.

You need to start with you. It's called organization. You need to organize your life to increase your productivity, finance and health. I will talk about organization throughout this book.

I remember when I was working at Office Max for minimum wage. I was working eight hours a day on my feet and literally taking home something like one thousand-two hundred dollars per month. It was crazy. I remember my boss telling me that she had never used a resume to get a job. Maybe that's why she was in her mid-forties and working in customer service. I knew this wasn't what I wanted to do. I wanted to play music. I wanted to tour. I wanted to write records and become somebody. Years later, my focus changed and I wanted to build radio talk shows. So, I did. And within ten months of launching my first show, I was #1 FM Radio in Sacramento, California. Fast forward a few years and I would have over a dozen talk shows all over the country. I had talk shows popping up in Seattle, Denver, Miami and at one point had over a dozen radio talk shows in Sacramento. I was an instant success and it was because I put my mind to it and made something of myself.

Fast forward a few more years and I wanted to start writing books. The book you're reading started as one book and didn't sell, so I modified it with a different cover and it still didn't sell. Then, I modified it again and here you are now reading it with an entirely different title. You can never give up when you fail. You must always keep going and growing.

One day I came into work at my Office Max job, one of my co-workers said "hey, I saw you were showcased on Bearshare. I heard your music. Not bad." That was a huge accomplishment for me. This was an international website that showcased musicians from around the world. I knew about being showcased on the site, but never thought in a million years that a co-worker of mine at Office Max would see me online, listen to my music and acknowledge me as a musician. I knew at that point what I needed to be doing.

Immediately, I started booking shows at every venue I could. It didn't matter if it was local or out of town, for pay or for free. I knew I needed to be playing and producing and performing my music. I remember filling out so many time-off requests that the little box on my boss' office door was over flowing with days I couldn't work because I was playing shows somewhere and couldn't work. She came up to me one day and said, "you're going to have to decide whether you're going to work here or play music. You can't do both." I chose music and never looked back.

    This is a prime example of figuring out what you want to do and doing it. We all have something special inside of us. What are you passionate about? The biggest mistake people make when building a business is getting into business to make money. What they don't understand is that money is nothing more than the exchange of value for value. If I provide you with value and am able to help you get what you need to get done, then you'll give me what I need. If you get into business to chase money, you'll never provide the value needed to make yourself successful.

Notes

What is organization?

Organization is nothing more than putting something in its place. For instance, let's start with something we all have, a closet. Start by putting your pants on one side and your shirts on the other side. Your socks will go in one drawer and underwear in another drawer. That's it! Really that's all it takes.

So, when I talk to you about getting out of your dead-end job, you need to start by organizing your time. It's your time and you need some of it for you!

I hear a lot of people with excuses, "I don't have time for this or time for that", but you need to think about what it is YOU need for YOU to be happy.

So, you get up in the morning, get the kids ready, go to work, come home, feed the kids, bathe them, get them in bed and you're tired. You follow this routine for years and years and never leave that dead-end job. So, try this! When you get home and your TV is on, get a piece of paper and make a list as long as you want of the things you would love to do for a living. Don't be foolish and say an astronaut. Though it can happen, that takes decades of training.

After you have created your list, check off the ones that don't really interest you. This is where you decide on what it is you want to do. Do you want to work in medical? Or law enforcement? What about clothing and fashion? Maybe photography? Or do you really love purses? Or fixing things? Every day, start putting a little time, maybe just a half hour a day into that goal. As you become more involved in it, you put more time into it. Get the kids involved. If they enjoy it, you increase your productivity and are spending more time with the family.

So, let's say you chose medical. There are plenty of online classes that work around your schedule and in a couple years, you'll have a degree to help get a job that you'd like.

Let say you wanted to start a business. In the back of your mind, you have always wanted to design clothing. You need to start by finding out what it is you want to do. That's not my job, that's your job. Then you need to DO. Start with making just a few pieces at a time. The kids will probably help you because when the clothes are done, they will probably want to wear them to school. Then their friends will see the new threads and want some too. As popularity builds, you start attending local trade shows and festivals. Usually those events are on weekends, so you don't have to take much time from work. All it takes is organization.

When I shut down my retail stores in 2012 after the recession took me for a loop, I had to organize myself and my life. I shut down the business, forfeited my apartment and took my little green Porsche and acoustic guitar to local coffee shops playing for tips and selling CDs. I took a job at Taco Bell making three hundred dollars every two weeks and immediately got to work building my next business, my media company. After a couple of months, I started selling cars and was homeless sleeping on a buddy's floor eventually choosing to open a small office and sleeping on the floor and brushing my teeth at a local Target store bathroom before heading back to sell more cars. Within a year, I was back on my feet and now working for a local mortgage company and still building my media company.

From January 2013 until July 2015, I was employed but building the new company. The day I left my job to pursue my media company full time was probably the best decision I ever made, with the exception of marrying my wife. Today, I have built an empire and this business will make me money for the rest of my life whether I work or not. I make money in my sleep. I make money when I am on vacation. I am always making money. I am going to show you how to do this.

Notes

Starting Your First Business

Starting a business is easy. And depending on what it is you want to start, it's fairly inexpensive. Small business loans are available if you want to open a small restaurant and investors love to get involved in new projects when presented to them, if it makes sense and you have done your homework. However, that's what they do, invest.

Now, I'm not saying anybody can start a business, because they cannot. It takes passion, determination, a lot of patience and a lot of hard work. Even though its hard work, it doesn't seem like it if you're enjoying what you do. So, how do you start your first business?

Here's an example.

You love purses. You walk into a store, see a cute purse and go OOOH, I want that. And usually you end up buying it. There are two ways to look at this? You work for somebody else, hate your job, but you're shopping for purses. Let's use that time and turn play into business. Let's say, you have no kids. You come home from work and plop down in front of the TV and your boyfriend comes over for dinner. A little snuggle snuggle. He goes home and goes to bed. That time could've been put to good use.

Companies all over the world sell purses.

Designer brands and no-name brands. Find a distributor that sells purses. You can do this by looking up Purse Distributors in a search engine. Call them up and ask them for a dealer application. Most likely you will need a business license and sellers permit before creating an account as a dealer with that distributor. Go to your local City Hall for the business license. It shouldn't cost you any more than sixty dollars. The seller's permit you can get from your Board of Equalization office. They usually don't cost anything. Once you get your permits, fill out the dealer application, send it to the distributor and viola. You're now a dealer. Now it's time to sell. Start small. Buy two or three to make sure the quality is there first. You don't want to sell junk to your customers. You'll make a couple of bucks, but they won't come back to buy anything else. When the product arrives, if you're happy with the quality, show it to your friends. You may sell a few or even more to your friends and family. When you have decided that you're 1) having fun and 2) making money, it's time to make a larger purchase.

Before you go any further make sure you're organized. You need a place to work. Do you have a place you can work and keep track of receipts, invoices and expenses? You need a small desk in the corner of your home that you can work and actually get things done. Make sure to hire a CPA or Accountant to handle your business finances. DO NOT try to do it yourself. You do not know what you don't know and tax laws change quite often, so hiring a professional is key.

You need to separate expenses from sales invoices and so on. Pick up a small business software package from your local office supply store or you can do what I did and build your own. If you put an hour a day into the business, after a couple of months you'll see a steady increase in sales if you build a solid foundation. I will talk to you about that shortly. The saying goes, a yard is hard, but an inch is a cinch. This means, just take things slow and make sure your business progresses each and every day.

So, you just got home from work and there is a big box on your porch that contains twenty-four purses. You can't wait to open it. What are you going to do with all those purses? That's easy! Sell them. Flea Markets, online classified ads and many other avenues are ways YOU can sell that product. Remember, the faster you sell them, the more money that goes into your pocket and quicker you can order more purses. You now own a business. Congratulations.

Another great way to move this inventory is build a website showcasing your product. Advertise the products on social media like Facebook, Twitter, Instagram and Pinterest. Drive traffic to the site using Google Adwords and other advertising options and if the product is competitive in price and of a designer brand with quality, the product should essentially sell itself. Most distribution companies offer drop ship programs where you can sell their products but only order once the product sells. They will pack and ship the item to your customer and charge you a small drop ship fee. This reduces operating costs and creates a much larger catalog of products increasing the odds of selling your products, making you more money in the long run. It's a lot of work, but you have to start somewhere.

Notes

Building My First Retail Store

I remember sitting at home one night and getting the crazy idea of opening a retail store. I already had dozens of online stores selling motorcycle gear and my apartment literally had hundreds of items I would be taking to local flea markets and selling on Craigslist. I literally had two to three people per day coming by my home to pick up gear, so a retail store was inevitable.

The first challenge was getting the capital needed and finding a good store front. Retail space is very expensive and the last thing we want to do is go out of business before we are actually in business. I scoured Craigslist looking at retail space and the cheapest place I could find was about eight hundred square feet and about one thousand two hundred dollars per month.

Building a retail store, you need to pay attention to ROI (return on investment). ROI is simple. If you invest one thousand two hundred dollars per month into a space, the space must create a return equal or greater to your cost of the space. My recommendation is two-to-one. Meaning, if you spend one thousand two hundred dollars per month, the space should create a return of two thousand four hundred dollars per month net or after expenses.

My decision was instead of opening a retail

store, I would rent some commercial office space for under four hundred dollars per month. The space was much smaller and in a strip mall, which was harder to find and less retail looking, but my return would cover the expenses of rent, electricity, internet, phone, etc. This was a smart move and an instant success for my customers. This was a safe bet in order to get started and learn the operation of running a retail store.

One of the biggest mistakes entrepreneurs make is reading books on business but never applying themselves or when they do apply themselves, they bite off more than they can chew and create a lot more risk that they can handle, which is the mistake I made with my retail stores. Years later, I look back and love the fact that I made the mistakes because of how much I learned and that I was smart enough and strong enough to bounce back and come back even more successful than before in a matter of a few short years.

Building retail stores was a challenge, but a fun challenge. I want to use the space below to show you how to properly design and build your business structure. It's all about leveraging your money and guaranteeing a return.

Product A: Cost $2.00 Retail $9.99 Profit $7.99
Product B: Cost $10.00 Retail $29.99 Profit $19.99
Product C: Cost $20.00 Retail $49.99 Profit $29.99
Product D: Cost $40.00 Retail $79.99 Profit $39.99
Product E: Cost $50.00 Retail $99.99 Profit $49.99
Product F: Cost $90.00 Retail $179.99 Profit $89.99

Above you see a variety of products with our unit cost, retail price and profit. Now a couple things I want to point out. Sales will obviously affect your profit margins, as well as theft, as well as taxes paid to IRS. You also have to factor in the cost of doing business, ie: Employees, Rent, etc, but this is a general idea.

Now obviously it makes sense to sell the more expensive item because you'll make more money on that item. However, not every customer wants to spend hundreds of dollars during one purchase. So, those clients will want a product of maybe a little lesser quality but something that will fit their budget. Now flipping the coin. There are customers who absolutely want the more expensive product and will pay full retail for it.

There are three types of customers. I call them the Dollar Store Customer, The Wal Mart Customer and The Nordstrom Customer. All three customers are shoppers and buyers in your store, however their wants and needs are different. The Dollar Store customer doesn't make a ton of money and wants whatever will get the job done for as little money as possible. The Wal Mart Customer wants a good product, not superior and wants it for a fair price. They won't buy the cheapest product but also aren't interested in the top of the line either. The Nordstrom customer may make the same money as The Wal Mart Customer but will take their time and buy the best they can get because they feel like they deserve it. Some Nordstrom customers make more money than The Wal Mart shopper and simply don't care about price. What does all this mean?

When pricing your products and building your store, make sure you have products available for each of those customers. You want all of them in your store. However, when that Nordstrom customer is buying your product, this is a fantastic time to upsell them with VALUE, meaning, you can sell them an additional product or products of lesser quality and they feel like they are getting more for less. This also works with your Wal Mart customers with small ten dollar add ones. By showing the benefits of accessories, both The Wal Mart and Nordstrom customer will most likely spend more on additional products. This increases your point of sale transaction amount increasing the health of your business.

Notes

Building a Foundation

As I said before, building a business is easy, but it takes time. To build a successful business, you need to build a foundation, also called a business system. This system is in place to ensure that every transaction goes smoothly and accurately. Without a system, the business will fail.

The system starts before you make your first sale. It starts with how you invoice your customer, how you enter the sale into your database and how you file the invoice after the sale is complete. Also, you need to keep track of expenses. A lot of people say it is okay to lose money your first year in business. I think that is all wrong. If you are already losing money your first year in business, then your system you have in place is failing you. If you lose money your first year in business, how will you survive five or ten or even fifteen years later? You can't.

Here's an example of how it should work. You order one dozen pair of sunglasses. The sunglasses cost you two dollars each. You want to sell them for ten dollars each. Ideally, you have a profit of eight dollars per pair, but no, you do not. Factor in shipping from the vendor to you. That was six dollars for the dozen, equaling out to fifty cents per pair. Your profit is now seven dollars fifty cents per pair. Remember, you still must pay for invoices, advertising, and a place to sell your sunglasses. If you are selling at the local flea market, then you need to factor in the expenses of the space you will be renting at the flea market. So, obviously if you take a dozen pair of sunglasses to the flea market, you will be losing money. But what if you took twenty dozen sunglasses to the flea market? Let's look at the figures.

With one dozen pair of sunglasses. Your cost is two dollars each. You sell all twelve pair at ten dollars each and take home one hundred-twenty dollars. Your cost plus shipping for the sunglasses were thirty dollars, the space rental was forty dollars and an invoice book is two dollars. After all was said and done, before taxes, you made forty-eight dollars. Not bad from money for a dozen pair of sunglasses.

Now let's get realistic. Nobody goes to the flea market with one dozen pair of sunglasses. More like twenty dozen sunglasses. And typically, sunglasses sell for about five dollars a pair at the flea market. So, let's look at the figures. Twenty dozen sunglasses at two dollars each will cost you four hundred eighty dollars. Shipping will be a little cheaper because of the quantity. Add about twelve dollars for shipping. You're at four hundred ninety-two dollars. You will need tables to display your products. That's about one hundred dollars. You're now at five hundred ninety-two dollars. Space rental at the flea market is forty dollars. Now you're at six hundred thirty-two dollars. The numbers add up quickly. Now let's start selling and have some fun. Now you probably won't sell every pair of sunglasses in one day, but let's say you did. After selling two hundred forty pair of sunglasses, you will have earned one thousand two hundred dollars. Now subtract your expenses of six hundred thirty-two dollars. Before taxes, you will have earned five hundred sixty-eight dollars. Not bad for a day's work. Take that money and buy more glasses. But remember, you only have to buy those tables once, so next time, one hundred more dollars will be in your pocket.

You don't have to only sell sunglasses. This was nothing more than an example. Whatever it is that you like, there is a market for it and you can make money selling the things that you love. I like music, so I write music, record it and sell it. I love motorcycles, so I build motorcycle and racing shops. I love cars, so I sold auto parts. Not only did I sell products at flea markets for years, I've also travelled to fairs and festivals, motorcycle and automotive events as well as online. I've owned dozens of websites that have sold tens of thousands of items to every corner of the world. I enjoy what I do and continue to wake up every day working in industries I love.

Notes

Personal Finance

Before you can start your first business, you need to get your personal finances in order. Balancing a checkbook is the very beginning. Being able to balance a checkbook is not easy if you have never done it, it takes practice. Like riding a bike. Once you get the hang of it, you can get creative to build personal wealth.

I have eleven banks. I started with one like everybody else and built to two and so on. I have several savings accounts and every account plays a different role. Whether it's for paying bills or saving money for something I want to buy or just putting away for my future. That money is there for protection. Money is power and without it, you're weak. Without money, we cannot eat or survive. So why live paycheck to paycheck? What if something breaks on your car? Are you going to use credit cards? I'm not. I have money put away just for that reason, IF something comes up.

Here's how to get started. Most of us already have a bank account. Get used to documenting EVERY SINGLE entry in and out of the account using Excel from Microsoft. If you don't have Excel, there are other Spreadsheet software programs available.

You start with your current balance. Every time you purchase something, take the receipt, put it into your wallet, NOT the bottom of your purse and when you get home enter it into your spreadsheet. Every night before you go to bed, you will know where every cent is going. Remember, organization. Most banks now have Online Banking. Online Banking is NOT ENOUGH to be organized. Take the extra step by creating a Spreadsheet. This makes things so much easier. Each night, make sure you have lined up every transaction with your online banking, make sure you enter the receipts that have not yet cleared, such as pending checks and restaurant receipts. When you get up, those uncleared transactions may have now cleared so again line up your online banking with your spreadsheet. You will at every moment's notice know every cent you have spent and know to the penny how much money is available in your account.

Now, let's start building wealth. If you don't already have a savings account, open one. Here's why. We are going to use your online banking as a tool to build wealth. Call or visit your bank and set up an automatic transfer program that will transfer a small amount of money from your checking account into your saving account on a regular basis. Let's start small, like five dollars a day. If you can do more, great!

If five dollars was pulled from your checking Monday thru Friday and placed into your savings, in one week, you would have saved twenty-five dollars. It may not seem like a lot. But here is where it gets fun. In only one month, you have saved approximately one hundred dollars. In a year, that is one thousand two hundred dollars. If you can transfer more each day, do it. Remember to pay yourself first. If you put that money into savings each day, you will find you have less money to spend on things like coffee and snacks from the vending machines at work.

So, if you apply both lesson one, starting your first business and lesson two, saving, think of all the extra money you will have. Just because you have extra money, it doesn't mean you need to spend it. As your savings grows, the interest the account accrues will increase. The more you make, the more you save.

Notes

Spenders, Savers and Investors

There are 3 types of people in this world. Spenders, Savers and Investors.

Spenders spend every cent they get, whether it's on newspapers or coffee at work. If they have it, they spend it. That is the absolute worst habit you can have. Savers save as much as they can and prefer not to use investment vehicles. Investors, save and spend. They spend on what they need. Then use the difference to save and invest in vehicles that will over time make them even more money. Stocks are a great vehicle to invest in. Many people say stocks are a risky investment, but so is spending every penny you get without a rhyme or reason.

Spenders:

Imagine if instead of spending money on "stuff", you took that money and put it to use in creating a sustainable business. How much do you spend on coffee in a year's time? If you bought one cup of coffee a day, five days a week, for four dollars per cup, you would spend one thousand-forty dollars in a year's time. Imagine if you were taking that money to buy product for your business. You could be turning that money into tens of thousands of dollars annually which then turns into even more money the following year, and year after and year after.

Savers:

Imagine taking that one thousand-forty dollars and multiply that by twenty years of saving. You have saved twenty thousand-eight hundred dollars. The problem is interest is only growing that money pennies at a time and inflation is actually eating away at the buying power of the value of this money. A lot of people have money put away, saved for years and years, but when it's time to start relying on this money, it's almost worthless. And most often times, there isn't enough money saved to actually live a quality and sustainable life. This is where investing comes in.

Investors:

How the rich get richer is having their money work for them. Robert Kiyosaki teaches Assets over Liabilities and this is how you want to handle your personal and business finances. If you build all of your business using the Asset to Liability ratio of 2:1 or greater, you will never run into a problem and will always maintain profit.

An asset is something that makes money month over month without you having to work for it. If you have rental income and your expenses are one-thousand dollars per month with rents at one-thousand four-hundred dollars per month, that is a lot of risk to make a little bit of money. However, if you're creating a brand that will make you ten thousand dollars per month, but only cost you three thousand dollars per month, that is a 3.3:1 ratio that creates wealth and sustainability.

Notes

Stocks

Stocks are a very fun and interactive way to build wealth that is yes risky, but only risky if you don't understand how the numbers works. There is a time and place for everything. So, how do you know when the time is right? Study the trends. Look at a company's history. Read the news. Look at products that companies are building for release in the near future. You must believe in the company before you buy a stock. If you do not, then how do you expect to make money if you yourself do not believe in the company.

You like cars. In 2009 the auto industry changed dramatically. Companies that had been around for one hundred years filed for bankruptcy. So, I'll ask you again. When is a good time to buy? As soon as that company pulls out of bankruptcy. The stock will be low. Buy it. Don't spend your savings. Only buy what you are comfortable buying. Remember that the broker will take it's share. It's usually a flat rate fee of about ten dollars per purchase. Buying or selling is called a trade. Remember, when you sell that stock or shares of that stock, they will charge you that same fee. As the market grows and demand increases on that stock, the price goes up.

It's a very simple formula. Demand goes up, price goes up. This formula follows us everywhere we go, whether it's the fuel pump or bread at the grocery store. So, when you're looking for that first stock, consider companies that are strong. Here's an example. Company XYZ has been in business for one hundred years. Their stock is currently twenty-five dollars per share. At ten shares, you will pay two hundred fifty dollars, plus the broker fee. We'll say it's ten dollars. So, you would pay two hundred sixty dollars for ten shares. With the fees included, you paid twenty-six dollars per share. This company has a new gadget coming out that the magazines and review companies are saying will be a big hit, such as the iPod, palm pilot, LCD tv, etc. Demand on these new products will drive the price of the stock up. That's what you want to look for. Three weeks after you bought your stock, the new product comes out and demand drives the stock to thirty dollars per share. Your stock, minus your fees has put forty dollars in your pocket. That's good. That's money. Congratulations, you just made money in the stock market.

Now find your next stock. We will go back to cars. During the recession in 2009, people were afraid of buying stocks in the auto industry. I made a lot of money in stocks during the 2009 recession purchasing stocks in the auto industry. There are a lot of companies in this industry other than manufacturers. There are dealership chains, rental car companies, maintenance and repair companies. These companies were thriving during this time. I bought a fair amount of stock in each company and sat back and watched the stocks grow. People have to drive cars and whether they are buying new cars or used cars, they also have to rent cars when they travel and have to maintain their cars, so they will last.

Also look at computer companies.

As our world gets further out of the industrial age and into the information age, communications companies will grow. Websites and media companies are making more money now than they ever have and these are also very good companies to consider. Remember to look at the trends and have faith in what it is the company is doing before you buy.

Notes

Using OPM

After you have created a nice stock portfolio, you can use OPM (Other People's Money) to your advantage. Let's say you spent a total of five hundred dollars in stocks and your stock is currently worth one thousand dollars. You can sell five hundred dollars of those shares to purchase more stock from either this company or another company. Those shares can make you even more money as the market grows.

When I was building The Good Life Show with Jon Robert Quinn, I had just been laid off from my job as a mortgage loan officer. See, I have a problem working for people. When I don't like something, I speak my mind. My clients know it and respect me for it. But, when you walk into your boss' office and speak your mind, you get to go home early and get paid early too. The problem is, you never get to come back.

Back to my story. Where was I? Oh yes, OPM. I had no money to invest into the creation of The Good Life Show. However, I had value. See, money is nothing more than the exchange of value for value. Meaning, when you have something to offer somebody, you can get what you want equaling the value. So, when I was approached to do a talk show, it was very expensive to create, and I was literally a couple days from just getting canned by the mortgage company. I knew however that I had something other people needed.

The radio station needed a thousand dollars per month for air time and I needed to survive. All I did was create value. I would approach businesses and sell them sponsor air time for five-hundred dollars per month. We could literally fit a half a dozen of these spots in a show and create thousands of dollars of passive income by giving them affordable air-time broadcasting their businesses to the community via the radio.

Within three weeks of being laid off or fired, whatever you want to call it, I was on the air, fully funded with sustainable income. Fast forward a year and The Good Life Show with Jon Robert Quinn was literally the number one show in Sacramento, California because we were providing valued to our clients.

To this day, I have never spent one penny of my own money on The Good Life Show. That folks is what you call OPM.

Notes

Encouraging Entrepreneurship

Running a business is different than being an entrepreneur. An Entrepreneur takes opportunities and thrives on them. He or she can literally take any situation and capitalize from it. A business owner basically takes a product or service and either makes a living with it or works part-time as a hobby. An Entrepreneur owns and has built many businesses and is well diversified in a variety of markets. A business owner plays it safe and works hard for his or her money. An entrepreneur takes calculated risks and works hard making sure his or her money is working hard for them.

I have always said that the term "entrepreneur" is extremely over used and it really takes away from how special "real" entrepreneurs are for our communities and society. Entrepreneurs are thinkers and dreamers. We are able to see things that don't exist and create them. We can look at an open plot of land and see a building in it's place. Or look at an empty shopping center and see the potential for opportunity. Or even look at an existing problem in our society and can see the solution to that problem. Furthermore, we can use intuition and create or bring the people together to create those concepts in our heads.

I hear sales people, drug dealers and people in

MLMs (multi-level marketing companies) call themselves entrepreneurs and it's pretty insulting in my honest opinion. Entrepreneurs are innovators. Entrepreneurs are the folks that make the cover of Forbes. I haven't seen many drug dealers, car sales people or MLM home businesses on the cover of Forbes.

I think the way to really tell a "real" entrepreneur apart from "the rest" is my term ultrapreneur. An ultrapreneur is somebody who has taken an original idea, brought the idea to market and has made in-excess of a million dollars from that idea. This divides the best from the rest. It also allows you to think clearly in finding the right people for your team. You never want to surround yourself with people who are lesser than yourself. What will make you successful is getting the right people on your team to take your idea to levels you cannot do on your own.

When building your team, you want to find the right people. As an entrepreneur, or ultrapreneur, you cannot possibly have control over every element in your business especially if you want to move from the S quadrant into the I quadrant. If you are trying to move from the I to the B quadrant, you absolutely must have your systems in place. Let's dig a little deeper into this in case you're not familiar with Robert Kiyosaki's Cashflow Quadrant.

Robert Kiyosaki teaches the most brilliant wealth formula I have ever seen. It's quite simple actually. I think what Robert is missing however is applying the system to your life. You have four quadrants. E for Employee. S for Small Business. I for

Investor and B for Big Business. In this you need to understand the asset and liability columns as well. I am only going to give you an overview of this model, so I recommend picking up a copy of Rich Dad Poor Dad from Robert Kiyosaki to fully understand his philosophy.

In order for you to grow wealth, you must first have been an employee to understand how the system works. From there you graduate to small business owner. Both the small business owner and employee quadrants are the highest worked and highest taxed quadrants. These are what I call the "have nots". The right side of the quadrant are the Investor and Big Business quadrants. The B and I quadrants are the "haves" and are the highest paid, most underworked with the least paid in taxes. This is because they understand Assets and Liabilities. You absolutely need to know this information if you want to become successful and wealthy as an entrepreneur.

An asset is something that makes money, night and day without you having to work for it because you have built it into a system. Real estate investments, royalties, leveraging money through other "safe" investment vehicles are assets IF they are making a positive ROI or return on investment. A liability is anything that takes money out of your pocket. So, when transitioning from the S quadrant to the B quadrant, you MUST go through the I quadrant first. In the S quadrant, you're a small business owner working for yourself, but the client is your boss. You're having to do EVERYTHING it seems and have no systems in place. If you're not sitting in the chair getting the work done, you're not making money. This is where you start building assets.

The book you're reading right now is one of my hundreds of assets. I have literally hundreds of intellectual properties that make me money whether I work or not. My books, my music and talk shows all produce revenue every single day whether I am asleep or awake. I am in the S and I quadrants because I still have to produce and distribute the product, however at the rate things are going, we are now building teams to handle to much of the work. I have to show up to record my talk shows because I have to be on camera and on mic and I also personally write the books or produce my music, but the team is taking control of the distribution of the product. I even have people handling my finances now. This is the transition from the I quadrant into the B quadrant. The B quadrant is when your system runs the machine and you can exit from the equation and the machine still runs without you. I hire the right people, people smarter than myself to do things I know little about or don't need to know. I just need to know that they are getting their job's done and we have enough revenue coming in to pay them for their work and allow me to continue creating new products and live the lifestyle I choose to live.

Personal wealth and growth flow around an entrepreneur. The passion, determination and drive for success is what makes an entrepreneur an entrepreneur. In order to be an entrepreneur, you must get creative, remove yourself from the box and get yourself ready for the ride of your life.

Notes

Be A Leader

When building a business, being a leader is most important, with the exception of the company's finances of course. When you're a leader, the employees and customers will respect you better than if you're the COOL guy. Whatever you do, do not be a push over. Being a leader doesn't mean you have to boss people around, but you must be a boss. You must be there as a mentor for your employees as well as love and respect each customer. If you're a micro manager, you will irritate your employees and lose their respect. If you're a bully, not only will you upset your employees, but it will bleed on your customers, in turn tarnishing the culture your business and hurt the company's reputation.

So, how do you become a leader without becoming a jerk? It starts with being respectful to your employees and understanding their wants and needs but also having good policies in place. Give people the benefit of the doubt. Don't but let them take advantage of you. Take interest in them. Get to know their families and their kids. For customers, giving a little freebee when it's within a few days of their birthday may cut into your bottom end, but will do wonders for repeat business, keeping you in business and increasing your word of mouth advertising. For your employees, on their birthday, give a $50.00 gift card for a night out on the town and have them take the day off. This will do wonders to the loyalty they have for your company. When they return to work, they may enjoy the atmosphere more and in turn will probably work a little harder. However, when they do wrong, show them what they did wrong and teach them the right way to get it done. If they keep making the same mistake over and over, maybe this isn't the best place for them.

When they need help or have a question, sit down and talk them through it. Show them that their hard work is actually appreciated. The best advice I can give is this, look at every boss you've ever worked for. Write down what you liked and didn't like and make sure that you provide your employees with what it was your past employers were lacking. Company growth starts from the top and rolls downhill. If you treat people right and set proper expectations, that behavior follows all the way down the chain with the end result being a happier customer. Happier employees means happier customers.

This brings me to an important point. When Andrew Carnegie was building the Carnegie Steel Company, he got to a point where he needed to increase the company's revenue. He brings in a rough and tough businessman by the name of Henry Frick to run operations. His less than orthodox way of running things left a sour taste in the mouths of the employees causing the Union to strike. After an intense battle, operations got back to business but not after several men lost their lives and ruined the reputation of Carnegie and his company. There was a right way and a wrong way to increase production and improve company profits. Unfortunately, the wrong choice was made here.

As a talk show host here in the Sacramento region, I work with a ton of local businesses and one that stands out to me is Nor Cal Auto Body. The owner Chad Riffe is innovative in his approach but loves his community and his employees and it shows in his work. He's got a thriving business and isn't afraid to step out of his comfort zone and take calculated risks to continue to build his brand and reputation. I love seeing businesses like this and there are a ton of them throughout the region. So, next time you're thinking about increasing productivity and revenue, look at yourself first and then your employee. It's a lot easier to keep your employees and clients happy than trying to find new ones when they leave.

Notes

Be Original

For your company to be successful, you must be original. You must think differently and open your mind to change. Being original entails thinking of new creative ways to accomplish challenges and building structure.

Originality means taking your craziest and wildest ideas and finding ways to make them work using your skills and tools. I love throwing ideas off people and getting their feedback. A lot of times, my ideas are so wild I just get a blank stare. I had an idea the other day for this community portal with marketplace, shopping, restaurants, community forum and business contacts for entrepreneurs in the community and the "suits" didn't understand why we would need something like this. The issue with this is because the area is booming and you've got to be ahead of the curve.

Once something like this is created by somebody else, there won't be much need for two of them. So, the one who gets there first wins and takes control of the marketing revenue from all of those businesses. The person I pitched the idea to was an employee in the E quadrant. They aren't an innovator and works twice or three times as hard as I work for half the money. Of course, they don't see the concept. I will probably move forward with the concept and then sell them the licensing rights once the platform is created. This is innovative thinking and the monthly or annual advertising revenue creates another asset for me.

Justin Bieber was original when it came to his hairstyle. Baskin Robbins was original by offering thirty-one flavors. Dodge was original by offering the Hemi. How are you or can you be different? When designing your business model, set yourself apart from the competition. Look at the issues in this world. It's a beautiful place is slow and look around you. But there are plenty of things that can use improvement and your talent set can provide a ton of value to those around you.

Remember money is nothing more than the exchange of value for value. If you can provide value to somebody, then they will provide you with what you need…money. You may be reading this book and seeing improper grammar, misspelled words, incorrect punctuation, but I never said I was an educated person. I am an entrepreneur with decades of experience that I share with those around me. I don't use ghost writers or proof readers. I like my products raw and real. When I produce my talk shows and even my music, I don't edit much, if at all. There are songs on my records that you can hear me hit the wrong note. I could have re-recorded it, but I didn't. Some would call that lazy. Ten years later, I listen to that recording and I remember where I was when I recorded it. I don't write music to sell records. I write music as an expression of my soul. I'm just lucky I have an audience that buys the music.

This is the same for my books. I have decades

of personal experiences as an entrepreneur with my many successes and failures and I write to share those with you, the reader to use these tools and lessons to better yourself and improve your business. Would you rather make all the mistakes I have made and learn the hard way or use my experiences and failures as an example of what to do and what not to do to? It's your choice. Maybe this will help you create something original.

Step One: Your product or service. Has anybody done it before you? If so, how can you make it better? If you cannot find a way to make it better, no matter how much you market the idea, it will always be second best. First, you need to find a want and need. If you have neither, then you have no market. Once you find the want and need, who is your targeted market? Try your product in other markets too. You'll be surprised at what you may find. When Honda released the Element SUV and marketed it to teens and young adults, they found that it wasn't the young adults buying and driving. Instead, it was the older crowd that found the Honda Element appealing.

Step Two: Your name. Is your name creative? Something memorable is key. Take your business name ideas and create a poll with some of your closest friends and family. Naming is important to the success of your brand or product, but remember, the decision is ultimately yours. If you don't have an emotional connection to it, don't use it.

Step Three: Marketing. Being original is very important when marketing a product or service. Maybe take the product and make it into a song or endorse a local charity or celebrity or restaurant to stand out from the rest of the crowd.

One thing I have done to be creative is, when I come up with something crazy, that I feel is genius, I present the idea to family or customers. If they say, "Hmmm, that might work", it's usually not as good as it could be. When I present an idea and they laugh at how ridiculous it is, I know I am onto something. Remember one thing. When you're onto something big, think bigger. I like to sit down and work out all the kinks, numbers, plans and if it works on paper, I run with it.

Take your business or service and think of ways you can be original. An example of a business I have come across lately that is completely original is All Area Real Estate. George Romonsky, a real estate broker in the local community as host of The Why Pay Six Percent Show, has built a real estate model only charging the seller one-percent to sell their home. Other agents in the area think he's crazy. Heck, even I have called him out, but in the end, he's selling more homes than the average agent. The public is happy with his product and his business thriving even when the markets are shifting for other agents. This is an example of innovation and creating a model that is original. Now it's your turn. How are you going to build an innovative and original business?

Notes

Building A Business System

Like I mentioned before, your business is like a child. Now, what keeps your child healthy is mainly the systems. The system is the engine that powers and maintains everything. The business system has many moving parts and each one of those parts must run in unison for the business to work properly. Every business should have it's core systems in place and must be followed or the business will fail.

A simple example of a business system is McDonald's. They have simple product, a simple price and are very convenient. However, what's behind the scenes of a McDonald's is one of the most complex business systems in the world. The reason why McDonald's works so well, is that each person has a task to follow. If at any point, the chain is broken, the system will stall. But even then, if each person follows procedure, the company will still operate efficiently.

These rules apply to your business too. Most small business owners are the salesman, the landlord, the accountant, the janitor, stock the warehouse, unload the trucks, place orders, ship orders, etc. Essentially, they created one really big JOB for themselves, not a business. For your business to grow, you'll need to hire people. That means giving up responsibility of some, if not many of the tasks. The problem you run into as a small business owner is that you have or will become a slave of your creation if it is not designed properly. You can do this by building a strong foundation. That foundation starts with getting the right people to handle each task appropriately.

For your new hires to do their jobs properly, you'll need to formulate a system. As you hire more and more people, this system will get more and more complex. For your company to run efficiently and profitable, your employee's responsibilities must be clear to be completed properly. One of the ways you can do this more efficiently is hiring private companies to handle different parts of your business. The marketing can go through an agency. The accounting can go through another agency. The packing and shipping can go through a fulfillment house. The online orders can go through a company that handles e-commerce systems. Then the cherry on top is the office manager that keeps everything running. This is a well-oiled machine if you're doing it properly. And, even though you own the business, you're not having to sit in the chair get to things done.

When I built my first business talk show, I knew I had to find clients to keep the machine running. I hired a media company to handle the production of the show. Then pay my clients a twenty percent referral fee for any business they send my way and with some transactions running three thousand dollars, six hundred dollars for sending a friend my way is a great way to keep those clients working with my organization. I hired a marketing agency to start shopping opportunities for more shows, creating new inventory and scaling the business out. I hired an accounting agency to handle my annual accounting. I have promotional companies handle getting the product out into the community. I started writing a business column for the local newspaper helping promote the shows, driving traffic to the machine. Then, I started writing business books and have teams and organizations handling much of those pieces as well. Now at thirty-six years old, I am looking at four-hour work days and a lifestyle most people experience from the pictures of magazine. A simple trip to my Instagram page will show you the lifestyle my wife and I live. We are happy and money is coming in through the systems we have built.

So, in relation to the body, every organ, every muscle, every cell, every part of our body serves an intricate purpose to ensure the machine runs exactly like it should. None of this would happen if it wasn't for the systems in place. Your business should be no different.

Notes

Expect Good Things

The saying goes you must give to receive. You must give respect to get respect. You must give love to get love. And you must give money if you want something in return. The same goes for your business. If you don't give your business one hundred percent, it won't give it back. My advice to any business owner is to love your business like a child. It's born, it lives, it thrives, and it even makes you proud. It puts a smile on your face. It makes you cry. It's a breathing, living, growing extension of you and someday, like everything in this world, it will die. But, like everything you do, if you love it, cherish it, raise it to be successful, it will love you back.

I remember when I was building my first business. It wasn't really a business at all but more so, was a part of me. I am referring to my music. From day one, I always thought ahead. I knew right out the gate marketing my brand as my real name would be almost impossible, considering my biological name is Robert Jones. I knew I needed to create something catchy. I needed to create something unique and it had to be timeless. I used names like John Michael Montgomery, a country singer in the 1990s and David Lee Roth, a rock singer from the 1980s as a reference. I came up with Jon Robert Quinn. I was seventeen years old at the time. I took Jon from Jones, Robert, my first name and Quinn, my mother's maiden name creating the brand that everybody knows today. This was just like naming a child. I knew that this journey would be a long one and I was in it to win it.

Throughout the years, I have owned retail stores, written several books, produced a ton of music, built talk shows, appeared on television, even did a little acting, and everything has been under the name Jon Robert Quinn. Why is this? There are two reasons really. One is because I am passionate about my business and the second reason is because rebranding yourself takes a lot of time and energy and getting that message to the community is very expensive.

I think one of the most expensive things in life is education. I am not talking about a college education, though that is very expensive as well, but more so talking about the lessons we learn in life. We make mistakes and that sometimes costs us a lot of money, relationships, even marriages. Your business has the same trials as life. I think one of the biggest mistakes people make with their business is not taking it serious enough. A lot of people are afraid to take that leap of faith and go all in. They have one foot in and one foot out. A lot of times they have a part-time or even full-time job as well. A lot of times I will tell an entrepreneur to quit their job and climb into the trenches. Getting into survival mode and not being able to make rent or even eat builds character and makes us THINK. Without thinking, we cannot succeed.

I work with a lot of local businesses hosting business talk shows in the region. I currently host nine shows in Sacramento alone and currently work with over two hundred local businesses. I see a lot of what business owners go through. I see the mistakes they make. I know who's making money and who isn't. I even know who thinks they are making money but will most likely be out of business in the next couple of years because they don't have the proper foundation set for their business. Too many people are trying to perfect the hamburger without getting the product out to the community and building a following. One business I am very impressed with is a company called Detoxination Wellness Centers. These guys have a unique product and are not only innovative, but are using science to give people an all-natural approach to become healthier.

What I find most appealing about working with these people is the fact that dad created this system, implemented it, built it into a sustainable model and the son now is taking the company to the next level. It doesn't stop there. These fine folks are creating helpful tools for people all over the world, creating new streams of income and reaching more people to help more people. This is loving your business like a child and creating a model that is sustainable for generations.

When your first child was born, what did you expect? You expected good things. You want your child to succeed. You want your child to fall in love. You want your child to someday make a child of their own, move out on their own and care for themselves. That is no different than a business. If the business is raised properly, it will outlive you. If raised properly, someday it will take care of you. If raised properly, it will branch out into other smaller businesses and someday grow into something as strong as its daddy.

So, when starting your first business, love it like a child, give it everything it needs and expect good things.

Notes

Properly Training Your Sales People

I see too many sales organizations today pushing for more sales people rather than making their current sales people better. It is very expensive for a sales organization to hire new sales people to bring better results and then firing the weaker sales people only after a month or so of poor production. This is honestly like throwing your old TV away because there is nothing to watch.

I remember years ago when I first got into sales. My first sales job was at Samsonite in Vacaville, California. I was seventeen. I would ride my bike nine miles each way back and forth to work. If it rained, I would wear a waterproof suit with my slacks, button-down shirt and tie underneath. After a long shift, I would typically change into my other work clothes and head on over to my graveyard shift security job at an auto parts distribution facility. I wasn't very good at sales, but I was a hard worker and my boss admired that. I showed up on time, did the best I could do and went home. After a few months, I found it wasn't for me and quit.

Shortly after this stint, I realized I was ready to officially start my first business. Again, I wasn't very good at sales, but I was a fast talker, a thinker and was innovative. After about a year in business, I found myself in a little bit of trouble and shut it down. I was now nineteen. A couple years would pass and I'd get a job at a car dealership selling cars. I only lasted about month here before I was let go. Why am I telling you this? My sales managers admired my hard work, but they never sat me down and taught me HOW to properly talk to people. All they taught me were shady sales tactics and scripts. This is how most sales organizations are run these days.

There are plenty of sales training classes and seminars out there and from what I have found, these courses are teaching sales people to memorize scripts. This is NOT how you train sales people. Sales really is just thinking on your feet and being great at your craft of problem solving. You cannot teach people a script to solve common problems on the sales floor. In addition, poor sales performance comes from lack of interest or just being crapped out. I believe that most sales people are really good at their craft but the organization itself is what is harming the sales and performance of the sales people. Poor pay, poor marketing and the organization not having the right focus in mind spins the sales person's mind, impairing their ability to sell.

Sales organizations put fear in sales people and with sales being a mental-based business, the sales person gets in their own head and literally paralyzes their ability to close the deal. Unfortunately, most sales organizations today lack in the uplifting and positive environments and are most focused on their bottom end resulting in cut backs. I went back and sold cars again in 2013. I had just shut down my second business and was pretty much homeless. I took too many calculated risks with my retail stores during the recession and couldn't pull out of it, like most entrepreneurs in that time.

I pull up to Sacramento Dodge in my Porsche with my laundry basket in the bonnet. I sit down with the sales manager and explain to him the situation. He asks where I live. I look over at my car. At this time, I am thirty years old, in a suit, my old beat up Porsche parked outside and looking for a sales job. I had already made my first million with my previous business, but like most people after the recession, I was broke. They hire me on the spot. Within a couple of weeks, I am at the top of leaderboard. A couple months would pass and I am spun out like the rest of the sales people complaining that the leads are weak, like from the movie Glengarry Glen Ross. The leads weren't weak, I was weak and the organization was breaking us. A few months later, the dealership was bought out by another company and everybody went separate ways.

At this point, I found myself working at Paramount Equity Mortgage. Say what you want, this was a wonderful and eye-opening experience for me. I feel like this organization made me the sales professional I am today. Without these hard-working people, I wouldn't have had the training and support I needed to become successful. I will say however that as their sales expectations grew within the company, so did the stress and our quality of life. Why was this? It was simply because they were hiring more and more sales people and had to cut corners in the training of the staff, affecting the quality of the employees brought on board. Yes, the company made more money, but also resulted in many class-action lawsuits costing the company millions of dollars long after those employees found employment elsewhere. It's not uncommon for me, years later, to open the mailbox and get another five hundred-dollar check from a class-action lawsuit.

Another huge mistake management takes today is overworking their sales people. I see sales people working ten, twelve or more hours each day to hit their quotas. This may seem productive because they are working more hours, but the mental fatigue ultimately is making a lot of those hours useless also causing them to resent their jobs. Management can properly train and encourage their sales teams to get the results they would expect, allowing the sales people to work less hours, enjoy their jobs, spend time with their families and giving the organization less turnover.

So, my advice is this. If you're starting or currently running a sales organization, you need to sit and speak with your employees, have empathy and find out HOW you can better their lives. People are NOT motivated by money. They are motivated by family and what that money can do. So, instead of spiffs and one hundred-dollar bonuses, maybe a day off and dinner out on the town with their spouse is a better approach. They come back to work refreshed and ready for another productive day.

Notes

Happiness

I have heard money doesn't bring happiness. Neither does being broke or poor]. Do you know the difference between being broke and poor? Poor people are poor forever. They are born poor and die poor. Broke people have money either put away that they refuse to spend, or an event has happened making it difficult for them to keep that money. Being poor is eternal. Being broke is temporary. Use these tools in this book to build your financial outlook. It's okay to be broke, because it means you are hungry. You are eager to build wealth and want to work hard to get to that goal of achievement. Do what you feel is right in your life. But, make sure your attention isn't spent on spending because you're sad or depressed.

Referring back to purses. You hate your job. Your life is so drab. When you're sad, don't go out and buy a purse. Instead, build a business to get you out of that dead-end job and sell those very same purses to others to build your wealth and future.

If you look around you, you will see people broke and happy and rich and sad. Why is this? I am not psychologist, but my guess is that their priorities are in the wrong place. Why are rich people spending to fill voids and poor people happy around family? Why do rich people work on Christmas and not at home with their families? As an entrepreneur, I think it is very important to understand the balance of greed and contentment.

Money does very interesting things to people. Until you have a lot of it, you won't realize the effects it has on you. When I got rich, I started spending and buying all the things I always wanted. At one time I had a dozen high-end watches, a Porsche, two BMWs, high rise penthouse apartment, thousand-dollar designer suits, expensive wines and memberships everywhere I could to make myself feel important. Shortly after, I found myself broke again and falling behind on repair bills for my high-end cars. Today, I make the same money, have the same assets but have one nice watch and drive a Mini Cooper. I realized that it's not the shiny things that make us rich, it's our quality of life and what our life means to us.

A lot of people want to be rich and wealthy. But what a lot of people don't realize is that they aren't the same thing. Rich is a quality of life and wealth is measured on a scale sustainability from your asset column. If you have built a successful asset column that pays you well and allows you sustainability of a two-to-one or greater ratio, then you will not only be rich but wealthy. However, if you're miserable and always chasing that shiny object, you may be wealthy, but will never be rich.

Notes

Conclusion

I think the most important part of building a business is staying Green. If you're not Green, meaning eager to learn and grow, you're dead. Get out of the business and move on. For over twenty years, I have built successful and unsuccessful businesses, but that's what entrepreneurship is all about. We come up with ideas all the time and try them. Sometimes we do well. Sometimes we fail. But with every success and failure is a lesson. Nobody ever said an education wasn't cheap. Some people go to college and get a degree and find a job. Others, like myself, never went to college. We just dabbled in this or that until something worked and stuck with it until it didn't work anymore, then went onto something else. Essentially, that's all business is.

Enjoy being an entrepreneur. Learn. Grow. Adapt. Innovate. And as my father always told me, use your head not your back. It's quicker to get it done right the first time, than having to do it twice.

Notes

Notes

Notes

Notes

Other Titles by Jon Robert Quinn

Books

- The Cold Call King: How to Make More Effective Sales Calls

- One Long Road: My Journey as a Musician & Recording Artist

- Being Quinnessential: Beginners Guide to Becoming a Gentleman (2018)

- Searching for Sara (2017)

Music

- New Faces (2000)
- Solo-Fisticated (2004)
- One Long Road (2004)
- JeRQ THIS (2005)
- Live '05 (2005)
- JeRQ THIS TOO (2006)
- The Road to Hammerlane (2006)
- A New Beginning (2007)
- The Best of Jon Robert Quinn (2008)
- One Day at a Time (2009)
- JeRQ THIS 3 (2010)
- 1982 (2015)
- The Best of Jon Robert Quinn: Vol 2 (2016)
- Made in England (2017)
- Quinnessential: 20 Years (2018)

Talk Shows

- The Good Life Show with Jon Robert Quinn (2015)
- 60 Minute Success (2016)
- The Cash Cow Show (2017)
- Why Pay Six Percent Show (2017)
- Investor Profits Now (2017)
- Real Estate Investor Weekly (2017)
- Women's Wealth Warrior Show (2018)
- The Jon Robert Quinn Show (2018)
- The Everyday CFO (2018)
- The Body by Vlad Show (2018)
- License to Kill (2018)
- Your Perfect Home (2018)
- Get Detoxinated (2018)

www.ingramcontent.com/pod-product-compliance
Lightning Source LLC
Chambersburg PA
CBHW030031250526
45464CB00025B/1033